THE BOY WHO BIKED THE WORLD

On the Road to Africa

ALASTAIR HUMPHREYS

ILLUSTRATED BY TOM MORGAN-JONES

Published by Eye Books

Published in 2011
by Eye Books
29 Barrow Street
Much Wenlock
Shropshire
TF13 6EN
www.eye-books.com

Second edition 2014
Revised 2015

ISBN: 978-1-903070-75-8

British Library Cataloguing in Publication Data.
A catalogue record for this book is available from the British Library.

Printed by CPI Group (UK) Ltd, Croydon CR0 4YY.

For Tom

CONTENTS

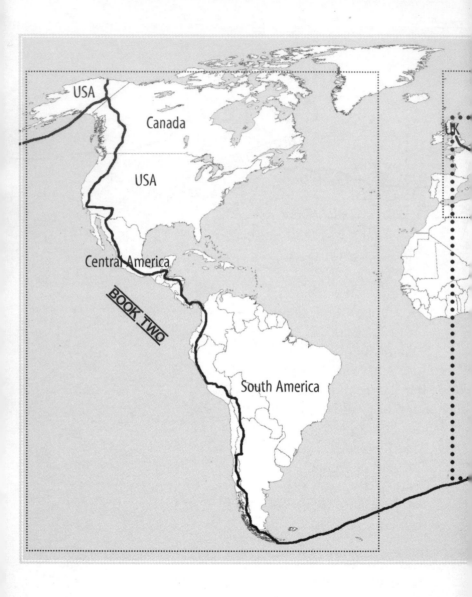

Tom's Route Round the World

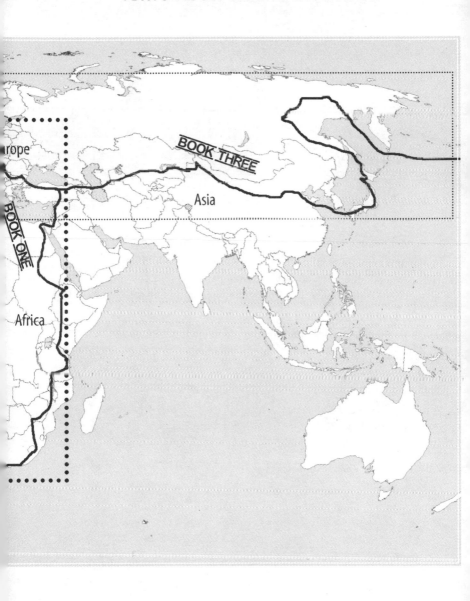

THE MAASAI ARE MASSIVE

Tom forced himself to keep smiling as the chief handed him a bowl of steaming blood and milk.

Circled around him, on the hard red earth, in the shade of a thorny African tree, sat 10 tall Maasai warriors, dressed in red robes and dangling earrings. In their hands they held long, sharp spears. They were looking at Tom with dark, shining eyes. Tom's blue eyes looked back at them. The spears glinted in the hot sunshine.

Tom looked away from the men and down at the carved wooden bowl. The mixture of cow's blood and milk was warm and, as the disgusting smell of the blood reached Tom's nose, he had to fight his stomach not to be sick.

"Pretend it's strawberry milkshake!" he pleaded silently to his stomach with his smile super-glued to his face. "Just pretend it's a milkshake ... "

And with that he gulped down the whole pink bowlful in one go. The men raised their spears in the air and cheered. Tom put down the bowl and wiped his chin.

As the grinning chief patted Tom on the back, Tom sighed with relief. This short ceremony meant that Tom was now welcome in the Maasai village. He would be safe here and everyone would look after him and make him feel welcome.

"That wasn't so bad after all!" he thought to himself. "Still, I should be used to swallowing weird food and drink by now."

The ceremony was over. "That's a funny sort of welcome," thought Tom. "Remind me never to be unwelcome here!" The men stood up and guided Tom back through the village. Their bare arms rippled with muscles. They walked together past huts built with branches, twigs, grass, and mud. Chickens scratched the dusty earth, searching for food. Tiny children stared in amazement at Tom, the strange new visitor to their village. The sun beat down. The men were all laughing and chattering together about Tom's performance drinking the traditional bowl of milk and blood. Tom could not understand their language but he saw that they were happy.

They led Tom to a flat piece of ground where he could set up his tent for the night. He felt happy. He was tired after another long day's ride. But he had made new friends in this village, and he had a good place to put his tent for the night. Plus, he was having a real adventure.

Tom thought of his friends back home, wondering what they were doing right now. What would they think if they knew that Tom had ridden his bicycle all the way to Africa?

He didn't think that they would believe him. Would you believe that someone could ride his or her bike all the way to Africa? But it was true, all true. Tom finished putting up his tent and unrolled his sleeping bag. Then he thought back to how all this began ...

DAYDREAMS OF ADVENTURE

Sitting at his desk at school Tom always used to stare out of the window and dream of adventure. He wanted to be an explorer! He daydreamed about the wonderful places in the world that he had read about in books or seen on TV or on the Internet. How exciting it would be to stand on the Great Wall of China and stare out towards the wilds of Mongolia. It would be brilliant to watch grizzly bears fishing for salmon in Alaskan rivers. He wanted to eat Chinese food in China, noisily slurping noodles with chopsticks. Think of a country in the world – any country – and you can be sure that Tom had dreamed about it. Tom wanted to go to every single country in the world. And as there are around 200 countries in the world he knew that he had to get started soon.

Tom could hear birds singing. He could not hear the teacher any more. How lovely! Undisturbed dreaming ... Gradually, though, Tom noticed that the room had gone quiet. Too quiet. With a burst of embarrassment he suddenly realised that the whole class was looking at him. He jumped in his seat. No longer was he battling through the rainforest.

He was back in his Maths lesson. And the teacher was waiting for an answer. Oh dear!

"Erm ... I don't know." Tom mumbled, blushing.

"You don't even know what the question was, Tom, do you?" demanded Tom's teacher. He was fed up with Tom's daydreaming.

"No, I don't know what the question was. Sorry!" apologised Tom.

He liked Mr Field and didn't want to make him angry. It wasn't Mr Field's fault that Tom was a daydreamer.

"So, where in the world were you dreaming of this time?" asked Mr Field, his voice rising and his face turning pink with annoyance. "Timbuktu? The North Pole?"

Some of the class sniggered.

Mr Field continued, waving his hands in the air in frustration.

"I am **sick** and **tired** of having to repeat **everything** I say to you because you are **thousands of miles away** in the **Amazon jungle**. You're on long distance quests when you should be doing your long division questions!"

The kids at the front of the classroom were enjoying this. Watching the teacher turn as red as a beetroot was more fun than doing their work. Every minute that Mr Field spent shouting at Tom was one minute closer to the end of the lesson as well.

And then it happened. He had certainly not planned it, he didn't know what made him do it, but suddenly Tom heard himself saying out loud,

"I am going to be an explorer! I am going to go round the world."

And everyone laughed.

Even old Mr Field laughed.

At that moment the lunch bell rang, saving Tom from further embarrassment.

TOM'S JOURNAL

WHERE I WANT TO GO AND WHY:

RUSSIA: **biggest** country in the world

VATICAN: smallest country in the world

MT EVEREST: highest mountain in the world

DEAD SEA: lowest place in the world (except for under the sea)

TIMBUKTU: because it sounds cool

ARCTIC: to see a polar bear

ANTARCTIC: to see a penguin

ANGEL FALLS: tallest waterfall in the world

~~MAMMOTH CAVE: biggest cave~~

AUSTRALIA: to see kangaroos & koalas

CHINA: to see the famous Great Wall

It is really difficult to write a list of places I want to go and why.

I want to go everywhere!
I want to see everything!

I want to swing on vines through the rainforest with monkeys in the Amazon. I want to ride a camel through the desert in Egypt. I want to feed the llamas at Machu Picchu.

Mum and Dad always tell me that anything is possible and I believe it !!!

I can cycle round the world. I can see all of these places. It will be hard, it will be scary, but I'm ready. I know that whatever happens, it will be worth it to ~~see~~ see all that the world has to see....

- Eiffel Tower
- Mayan Ruins
- Pyramids of Giza
- Statue of Liberty
- Taj Mahal
- Grand Canyon

I'm starting to think that my journey will be easier than writing this list. I should write a list of places I don't want to go: it would be a lot easier!

Tom

I AM GOING TO CYCLE ROUND THE WORLD

Circled around Tom in the school playground were a group of boys and girls from Tom's class. Other children, noticing the crowd, had gathered as well to see what all the excitement was about. They were looking at Tom with teasing, bullying eyes. Everyone was laughing. Everyone except Tom.

Tom looked away and down at the ground. He didn't like being in the middle of this crowd. He wanted to be left alone.

"How will you travel round the world? You haven't even got a car!" laughed one girl, Helen. She was always trying to annoy Tom.

Ever since Tom had told Mr Field that he was going to be an explorer, everyone had been laughing at Tom. He didn't like it. Nobody believed that he was really going to go round the world. Of course they didn't, it was a crazy idea. But now Tom was too embarrassed to say that he hadn't really meant it. He had been having a good old daydream and the words had just popped out. So he began defending himself instead.

"I've got a bike. I'll go on that! It will be the best bike ride ever!" replied Tom. "I'm going to cycle round the world."

"Yeah, but what about the sea? You can't ride your bike over the water!" teased Toby.

"I'll cross the seas on a sailing boat."

"You haven't got enough money to cycle round the world!" said someone else.

"I'll sleep in my tent and eat the cheapest food," replied Tom. "That way the trip won't be expensive."

"It's too far!"

"The mountains will be too high!"

"The deserts will be too hot!"

"The winters will be too cold!"

Everyone in the crowd shouted their reasons why it was impossible to cycle round the world.

It was a funny thing, but the more that people told him it was impossible, the more Tom found himself wanting to prove them wrong.

Nobody ever thought that Tom could do anything.

He was a shy and quiet boy. He wasn't the strongest or the fastest or the cleverest in his class. He was just normal. A lot of the teachers in the school didn't even know his name. But that did not mean he couldn't do amazing things as well. He began to believe that maybe it was possible to cycle round the world. He would dare to live his dreams, he would prove everyone wrong. And he would have a lot of fun at the same time!

— ✗ —

After school Tom ran all the way home and burst through the front door, completely out of breath.

"Hi Dad!" he yelled with excitement, "I'm going to ride my bike round the whole world!"

"That's nice, son," replied his Dad, who was peeling carrots at the sink. "I'll make you some sandwiches to take with you."

Still panting, and without even stopping to take off his coat, Tom ran upstairs to find his Mum.

"Mum, Mum! Where do we keep the tent?"

"You don't need the tent, Tom," she replied. "You need to do your homework."

So for what felt like the hundredth time that day Tom had to explain his plan – to set off from their front door and pedal on, on, on in an enormous world-wide circle until he arrived back home again.

"Well in that case, you will certainly need the tent," replied his Mum. "Why don't you write down a list of everything you need to take, and then I will help you pack."

For the first time that day Tom felt happy. At least his Mum and Dad hadn't laughed at his big plan. He ran to his bedroom.

Tom took out his diary and wrote neatly along the top of a new page: 'Things I need to take on my trip round the world'.

He looked around his room and saw his computer on the desk. He would definitely need that. His Mum and Dad would appreciate an email every now and again.

He listed all of his favourite T-shirts, a few pairs of jeans, and two pairs of trainers; one for cycling, and one for special occasions. Tom didn't know what the special occasion would be, but he was proud to be prepared.

He reached number eight on his list, and looked around his room again. He saw his guitar sitting in the corner. Yes, he would need his guitar.

Tom felt a bit silly for forgetting to include his bike until number nine, and forgetting his tent until number ten. But he was pleased with himself when he remembered his globe, which would help him find his way around the world. He was about to continue with his list when the door flew open and a blur of blonde energy burst into the room.

"Don't you ever knock?" shouted Tom at his little sister who had jumped onto his bed.

"Sorry!" grinned Lucy. She did not look very sorry at all. "But Mum told me you are going to cycle round the world! That is so cool. Can I help you? Please ... "

Tom realised he would miss Lucy when he was away. He wiped the scowl off his face and shuffled across the bed to make space for his sister.

"Sure," he said, "You can help. Mum told me to make a list of what I want to take with me, but it's hard: I want to take all of my things."

Lucy took the list from Tom, read it, and started to laugh. Everyone was laughing at Tom today and he was sick of it. "What are you laughing at?" he huffed, snatching the list back.

"Sorry," said Lucy, who did look a bit sorry this time. "But your list is crazy. You can't take any of that stuff: how will you carry it all?"

"But I love my computer," grumbled Tom.

"You need to take only what you really, really cannot survive without."

"I can't survive without my DS!"

"Tough," answered Lucy, her mouth serious under her curly hair, blue eyes and round cheeks. "You will soon be camping in a desert, visiting the pyramids, whizzing down mountain roads. Don't you think that is even cooler than computer games? Anyway, there's no electricity in the desert."

Tom sighed. His sister was right, as usual.

"Come on," encouraged Lucy, "I'll help you. Let's do it together."

And they got to work.

After they had written the list, the final thing that they needed to do was to work out the route that Tom should take around the world. Using a map of the world printed from the Internet they worked out an exciting route around the world.

Tom knew that he would have to solve lots of problems during his journey (such as trying to find boats to carry him across the oceans), but he thought it best not to worry too much about all those things right now. He didn't want to get so worried that he became too nervous even to begin his adventure!

At that minute Dad shouted up the stairs that their tea was ready.

THINGS I NEED TO TAKE
on my trip round the world
by Tom (and Lucy)

1. Bike
2. Dad's panniers (special bags for carrying things on a bike)
3. Tent
4. Sleeping Bag
5. Camping stove, pan, ~~fork~~ spoon
6. Water bottle
7. Two sets of clothes
8. Raincoat
9. One pair of trainers
10. Tools to fix the bike
11. Puncture repair kit & pump
12. Helmet and bike lights
13. Torch
14. All the money from my piggy-bank
15. Map and compass
16. Passport
17. Camera
18. Diary
19. Teddy Bear
20. Toothbrush

I printed out a map of the world and drew on the route I've decided to take to get to the end of Africa:

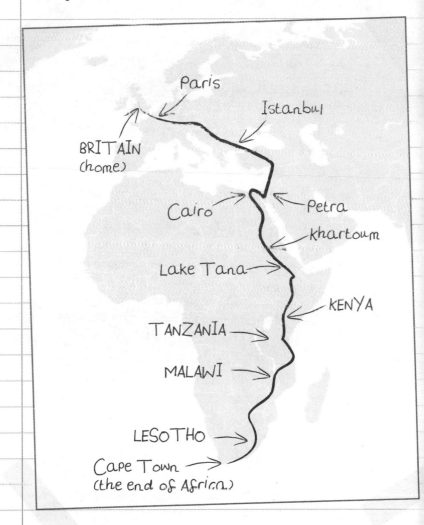

WHICH WAY TO AFRICA?

Tom woke up early the next morning and jumped out of bed. That was his last night sleeping in a soft bed for a long time. He was very excited about setting off on his adventure. All his bags were packed and he was ready to go. But he was nervous too. It felt like there were butterflies fluttering around inside him. Tom was sad to be saying goodbye to his family. He would miss them, but he knew that if he was going to be an explorer then he had to get started. He thought of Mr Field and all the children in his class. They didn't believe that he was actually going to do this. If he didn't start today then he would have to face everyone laughing at him again back at school. That gave him the final boost he needed. He was ready to ride.

"Which way is it to Africa, Dad?" Tom asked as he finished his breakfast. He knew the way from his house to the shops, but not which road to take to get to Africa.

"Turn left at the end of the road. That is south, which is the way you need to be going to get to Africa," answered his Dad. "Keep heading south."

"You will need to look on your map and ask people to help show you the way as you ride," added his Mum.

"Thanks, Mum. Thanks, Dad!" said Tom. "Well, I'd better

get started, I suppose. Bye bye everyone! See you when I get home again! I'll send you lots of postcards, I promise!"

Tom put his helmet on and climbed onto his bike.

"Good luck, Tom!" shouted his Mum and Dad and Lucy together. They looked sad that he was leaving, but also excited for him heading off on his big adventure.

Tom began pedalling. The bike felt heavy with all of his kit strapped onto it. He wobbled a bit until he picked up speed. At the end of the road Tom turned left, as his Dad had said. He waved to his family and rang the bell on his bike. They were all waving like mad. And then they were out of sight.

All of a sudden Tom felt very lonely. The world was a big place and he was all alone now. Already he missed games of football with his Dad, his Mum helping him with his problems, Lucy's sensible advice, even old Mr Field and some of his classmates. Tears started to roll down his cheeks.

But Tom knew that being an explorer was going to be hard at times. He talked to himself to get over his worries.

"Sometimes I will be lonely and scared and wishing I was back at home. But most of the time I'll be having brilliant adventures. It will be worth it."

His excitement began to return and he felt the breeze blowing on his face.

"I'll be fine once I get going."

He pedalled as fast as he could and gave a big cheer.

The sheep in a field looked up as they heard his voice and watched as he zoomed past on his shiny, loaded bike.

Tom's journey round the world had begun.

ARE YOU CRAZY?

After a few days' ride Tom reached the English Channel. He was really tired. He had never ridden so far before. Last week he would have thought that riding the length of England was a long way. But compared to cycling round the world it was nothing at all. He couldn't believe how far he had already pedalled, but he was still in England.

Tom was beginning to realise that riding round the world was not going to be easy. Maybe that was why everyone had been telling him how hard it would be.

But he wasn't going to give up yet. It was time to cross the sea to his first foreign country. Tom checked that his passport was still safely in his pocket and then pedalled towards the ferry.

Tom found the ticket office and spoke to the lady there.

"Hello, my name's Tom. I am going to cycle round the world, so I need a ferry ticket to France, please."

"You're going round the world? On a bike? Are you crazy? That must be thousands of miles!" The ticket lady couldn't believe what Tom had just told her. Tom was beginning to wish that he received £1 every time someone called him crazy. He would be rich already!

"It's true." Tom said, and he patted the seat of his bike.

"Well, if you are mad enough to be doing that then the least you deserve is a free ferry ticket." And she pushed a ticket to France across the counter.

"Thank you!" exclaimed Tom, amazed at her kindness.

"Good luck!" called the lady as Tom wheeled his heavy bike towards the ferry, clutching his free ticket and his passport. The horn blasted and the ferry set sail.

A Frenchman in a smart uniform stamped Tom's passport. Tom looked at the stamp – the first one in his passport – and smiled as he thought of all the colourful visa stamps he would be collecting. He put his passport in a safe place at the bottom of one of his bags so that he would not lose it and then rode into his first foreign country.

Tom was excited but he had to concentrate hard. The people in France looked like the people in England, but he could not understand what anyone was saying. He could not read the shop signs and the cars were driving on the right hand side of the road, not the left hand side like in England. He made sure that his helmet was fitting snugly before he began riding. It was amazing how different things could be after just a short ferry trip.

But which way was it to Africa?

Tom wondered how many times he was going to ask himself that question. Then he remembered his Mum's advice to ask people for help. Sitting on a bench nearby was a lady with a baby in a pushchair. Tom thought that she looked nice. He decided to ask her.

He rode over to the lady and asked politely,

"Excuse me please, can you tell me the way to Africa?" The lady looked at him, puzzled, and said nothing. Tom tried again.

"Excuse me please, can you tell me the way to Africa?" This time the lady said something, her shoulders shrugging and her hands waving as she spoke. Tom did not understand a word she was saying. It sounded like, "Ooh la la! Blah blah blah! Waffle wiffle wuffle."

Was that really what she was saying? Surely not. Unless she was crazy. Was she a crazy lady? She didn't look crazy. Of course! Tom realised she was speaking French. But Tom did not understand French. His class was not going to learn French until next year. Oh dear. He wished that Lucy was here. She would have a good idea. But just then he had a good idea of his own.

Tom rummaged in one of his bags and pulled out his map of the world. You don't need to speak the same language to recognise a map of the world. Every country has the same world maps. Tom showed his map to the lady, whose face seemed to suggest that she thought Tom was crazy. Tom pointed to the distinctive shape of Africa and then pointed down the street in both directions with a questioning look on his face.

"Africa?" he said once more.

The lady with the pushchair looked puzzled for a moment. Even her baby looked puzzled. She swept her brown hair from her face with her hand and asked,

"*Afrique?*"

"Africa." said Tom.

"*Afrique?*" said the lady once again, and pointed in growing amazement at Tom, then at his bike, and then back at Tom again.

Grinning, Tom nodded. This seemed to be going rather well.

"*Afrique,*" he repeated the French word for Africa. "That's an easy word to remember!" He made a pedalling motion with his hands to show that he wanted to cycle to Africa.

Shaking her head in amazement, she pointed left down the road, away from the setting sun, and said once again, "*Afrique.*"

"Thank you!" called Tom as he climbed back on his bike. He was so happy to be on his way that he forgot the lady did not speak English. He would have to start learning some French words, starting with 'thank you'.

Things were looking up. Maybe he wasn't actually mad to have begun this ride. He had crossed two gigantic hurdles already: he had left England and was into his first foreign country. And then, he had managed to communicate with somebody using sign language. And she had been friendly and helpful. Tom realised that he was not completely alone on his ride after all. He had everyone in the whole world to ask for help!

FRANCE

Tonight I pitched my tent in a park near Paris. I can see across the city, all the way to the beautiful Eiffel Tower.

So far I have seen so many cool things that I can't sleep. I just keep thinking about everything else I am going to see on my journey! I'm having lots of fun & seeing exciting new things every day.

At first I found it hard to talk to people, but it has got easier asking for directions. I've learned some simple French, but I've also used my hands to point at things & act out what I want. Actually this way is more fun ....

The other night I was offered snails and smelly cheese for tea! I ~~tr~~ tried everything, but I think I'll stick with my usual banana sandwiches - they're much cheaper too!

Tom

Words I've learned in French

(and need to learn in every other language!)

English	French
Hello	Bonjour
Goodbye	Au revoir
Thank you	Merci
Please	S'il vous plaît
Left	A gauche
Right	A droite
Straight ahead	Tout droit
Bicycle	Bicyclette
Africa	Afrique
Food	Nourriture
Water	L'eau

Bread is called a baguette

I don't have to learn numbers from 1 to 10 because I can just use my fingers for this!

HOW TO MAKE A BANANA SANDWICH AND OTHER VITAL LIFE LESSONS

Day after day Tom rode east across Europe. The days turned into weeks. The weeks turned into months.

He grew stronger and fitter each day. In the morning the sun was bright on his face as he rode towards it. By the evening the sun had moved round the sky and was behind him. Tom was pulled forwards by his evening shadow which stayed in front of him, encouraging him to keep going. He learned a few new words each day to help him talk to the people he met. He learned to put his tent up quickly without it blowing away. He fixed some punctures. And he felt the muscles in his legs growing bigger each day.

As well as becoming very fit, Tom realised that he was also hungry all the time. A hungry cyclist. Cycling uses up a lot of energy. He spent a lot of time daydreaming about food. It was in one of these early daydreams that Tom came up with the idea of banana sandwiches. They had lots of energy and they were very cheap. Tom lost count of how many hundreds of banana sandwiches he ate on his ride round the world.

Because he did not have much money, Tom always had to eat cheap food. He also liked to try the different foods in the countries he was riding through. But more often than not it was banana sandwiches in the day, noodles at night. The same thing day after day after day. This might sound a bit boring. But because he was always hungry, a banana sandwich or three tasted just as delicious as his Mum's best cooked dinners.

Another way that Tom kept his adventure cheap was by camping at night rather than staying in hotels. Sleeping in his tent was good because it was free. And it was good because it was exciting. It was bad because he could not have a shower so he got quite dirty. But Tom didn't care too much about that.

Each evening, as the sun began to set, Tom would look for a safe, quiet place to sleep. He would find a peaceful wood or a grassy field.

Once he stopped to camp he did the same things every time. First he would take off his sweaty shoes and socks. He liked the cool, fresh feel of the soft ground on his feet after a hard day's ride. As he could only get clean when he found a river to wash in, his feet were starting to become very smelly!

Next Tom set up his tent. He had a small green tent. It did not weigh much but it had enough space to protect him and all his things from the rain. The first few times he put the tent up he ended up in a complicated tangle of tent fabric and long poles. But he soon got the hang of it and now could put up the tent in just under five minutes.

Once his tent was up, Tom would find a nice log to use as a seat. Then he would cook his supper on his little camping stove. He did the washing-up simply by licking his spoon and wiping his pan clean with a piece of bread. He wondered if his Mum would let him use this new technique when he returned home. After eating, Tom would write his diary so that, even when he was an old man, he would never forget the adventures he had enjoyed that day. There are adventures every day if you know where and how to look for them.

BULGARIA

I'm sitting in my tent in Bulgaria trying to be really quiet. Animals only come out if they don't know I'm here. So far I've seen rabbits, foxes, and deer. But the most brilliant was the wild boar in a forest in Hungary. I hope I can see one of those again tonight, if I can stay awake long enough.

It's funny, I used to stay up really late to watch my television shows, but now after an exciting day cycling & seeing amazing things, I feel quite happy to sleep.

Some nights I can't even be bothered to put up my tent I'm so exhausted. But I still do, of course. I'll carry on towards Turkey tomorrow once I hear the morning birds singing.

Tom

1) My favourite foods !!!

I eat lots of banana sandwiches (recipe below!) but for a treat I eat food that is popular in each country.

Here's what I've tried so far:

- FRANCE: crêpes (thin pancakes) with chocolate & hazlenut spread
- GERMANY: sausages with curry sauce
- HUNGARY: goulash stew with beef & paprika
- AUSTRIA: wiener schnitzel (fried pork) with chips and loads of mayo!

RECIPE FOR BANANA SANDWICHES

1 Peel a banana
2 Put it on a piece of bread
3 Put another piece of bread on top
4 Push down hard on the sandwich to squidge the banana flat & spread it
5 Eat and repeat until full!

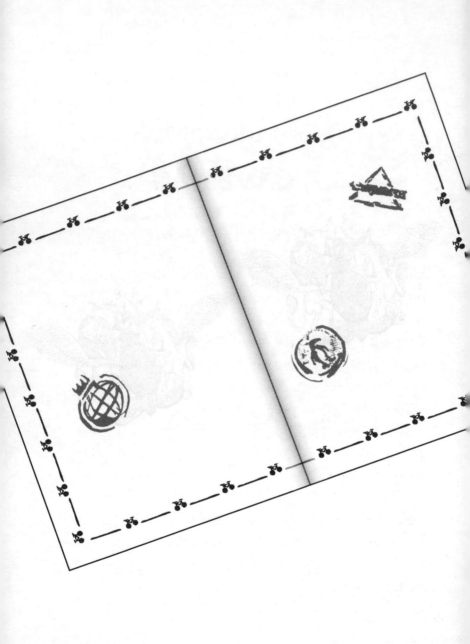

TOM BECOMES
A CAVEMAN

In the town of Donaueschingen in Germany (it took Tom about an hour of cycling before he managed to wrap his tongue round such a difficult name for a town) he had arrived on the banks of the mighty Danube River. The Danube, so blue, so bright and blue, is the second longest river in Europe (the longest river is the Volga in Russia). The Danube begins in the Black Forest of Germany (the forest famous for its cakes) and runs all the way to the Black Sea. It flows for 1700 miles. Tom was going to ride the length of it.

Tom sat munching his fourth banana sandwich of the day, and stared at the water sliding by. He felt hypnotised by the wide river. It had been flowing day and night, year after year for thousands and thousands of years. How amazing!

He rode alongside the River Danube for weeks, pedalling downstream through Austria, Slovakia, Hungary, Serbia, Romania and into Bulgaria where the Danube ran out into the Black Sea.

A few days after leaving Bulgaria Tom reached Istanbul. Istanbul is the biggest city in Turkey. It was also the most beautiful city he had been to so far. It has been an important city for thousands of years, and some of its most impressive buildings are very, very old. Tom wrote a postcard to his family back home.

After looking round Istanbul, taking lots of photos, and treating himself to some delicious *pide* (Turkish pizza), Tom rode down to the shore of the Bosporus. The Bosporus is a narrow strait of water about 700 metres wide, not far from Istanbul. Old men were sitting quietly on little stools holding fishing rods. They didn't seem to be catching many fish. But they didn't seem to mind either. They were happy chatting to their friends and feeling the warm sunshine on their faces.

The Bosporus marks the edge of Europe (the rest of Turkey is in Asia). Looking at the big ships sailing by, Tom was delighted to have made it right across Europe. His first continent was behind him. On the other side of the water lay a brand new continent. Even though Tom knew that Europe was the smallest and the easiest continent he would cross on his journey, he still felt proud. He was happy to have made it this far, but he was eager to keep going. New continents waited for him: new friends, new challenges, new adventures. Brilliant! Tom wheeled his bike onto the little ferry for the short ride across the water.

"Goodbye Europe! Hello rest of the world!" he shouted on the deck of the ferry into the breeze. A seagull whirled away in surprise at his loud voice, even though Turkish seagulls probably cannot understand English.

Riding through Turkey, Tom visited the region of Cappadocia. Two thousand years ago people had begun living in underground cities there. Homes, churches, store rooms: everything had been carved underground out of the rock. People had stored their harvests in caves, and kept their sheep and goats in them at night. Even today some people live in homes carved into the side of cliffs. As well as the interesting houses, Cappadocia also has weird, beautiful rock formations, known as fairy chimneys, that rise up out of the ground.

TURKEY

Today I saw a collection of jewel-covered swords in the Topkapi Palace in Istanbul. I also walked through the spice market. So many smells and noises and colours - much better than the supermarket back home! I've seen loads of amazing sights here, like Hagia Sophia, the biggest building in the world 1500 years ago! Since then it has been a church, a mosque, and now it is a museum.

And I couldn't believe the Blue Mosque! It was one of the most beautiful buildings I have ever seen with so many domes & ~~mida~~ ~~minaret~~ towers.

There was a family here in Turkey that lives in a super cool cave house near Cappadocia. It has electricity, a television, and a front door. They invited me to spend the night! On a proper bed! I think it was the best sleep

I have had so far. My sleeping bag can only cushion me so much. And I had a shower!

Since beginning this trip, I have become more observant. I've been learning so much about nature:
- Why trees grow so tall.
- Why the moon changes shape every night.
- Why rainbows happen.

I've also found out a lot of weird and interesting things about all of the cities I have cycled through in Europe. I found out that:
- Hot dogs were invented in Vienna, Austria.
- Dracula comes from Romania.
- In Bulgaria nodding your head means no and shaking it from side to side means yes!

The world really is an interesting place once you start to look at it properly!

SALAAM ALEIKUM!

After Turkey Tom rode into an area known as the Middle East, which consists of several different countries. The language of the Middle East is Arabic. Tom once again began learning new words. But he was faced with an extra difficulty in Arabic: even the alphabet was totally different. Suddenly shopfronts looked as though they had been splattered by spaghetti rather than words! His journey had just become even more difficult.

"How could all these squiggles be words?" thought Tom, helplessly. He could not even understand the road signs or distance signs because numbers are also written differently in Arabic. Tom had to use his fingers to explain how many bananas he wanted to buy when he pointed to them in shops.

Of course to the local people Arabic was easy and normal, and they would have found the English language just as funny-looking and difficult. Arabic is the fifth most common language on Earth, spoken by nearly 250 million people, so Tom thought he had better start learning.

The first thing Tom learned was how to greet people.

"*Salaam aleikum*!" shepherd boys shouted from the fields. In the mornings the people in the bakeries where Tom bought delicious, fresh flat bread (so hot he had to juggle it back to his bike), would smile and say *"Salaam aleikum."*

In fact every single person Tom met would say *"Salaam aleikum!"* to him.

Tom learned how to reply to this greeting which means "Peace be with you!"

He said *"Aleikum salaam"* which means "And peace to you also."

This greeting is used by every Muslim person in the world. A Muslim is someone who follows the religion of Islam. Islam is the second largest religion in the world and the biggest one in the Middle Eastern countries Tom was riding through.

Tom was on his way to Baalbek in Lebanon to see the largest Roman temples in the world. He had also been told about 'Hajar-al-Habla,' the biggest brick in the world which lay near to the temples. He definitely wanted to see that. The Romans had dreamed of building the ultimate temple, using bricks bigger than a bus! Tom couldn't even imagine how big this temple would have been. However, after carving the first giant brick out of stone in a quarry, the Romans realised that it was maybe just a bit too big. It weighed 1200 tons! So in the end they only made the first brick.

Baalbek was an exciting place. The temples were so well preserved that Tom found it easy to imagine Romans living there 2000 years ago. Six huge columns towered above him. Tom learned that eight more of the original stone columns had been taken down and carried by ship to Istanbul 1500 years ago. They were used in the building of Hagia Sophia which Tom had recently visited. This journey was teaching Tom how the history of so many different countries and cultures are all mixed up together.

The historic city of Petra in Jordan was even more astonishing. It took Tom about two weeks to ride there from Baalbek. Petra was another ancient city. Incredible temples and buildings have been carved into the side of cliffs. Although Petra was 2000 years old, people in Europe did not even know it existed until a Swiss explorer called Johann Ludwig Burckhardt re-discovered it just 200 years ago.

Petra is hidden away down a narrow, winding canyon. Tom pedalled down its winding route for about a mile. The steep rock walls rose up above him on both sides and he could see only a tiny slice of sky far, far above him.

"What an unbelievable entry to a city!" Tom thought to himself. "No wonder it stayed secret for so long."

But that was nothing compared to his excitement when he reached the end of the narrow gorge. Facing him, rising up from the sandy floor, was an enormous building carved out of the cliff known as the Treasury.

It was a beautiful rose-red colour. Tom's jaw dropped as he stared up at it. If people could make something so wonderful 2000 years ago then he could definitely ride his bike around the world. He was inspired to believe that he could actually do it.

THE MIDDLE EAST

Riding through the Middle East, I have learned a lot about the religion of Islam. Each year there is one holy month for Muslims, called Ramadan. It had just started when I got there. During Ramadan Muslims are not ~~allowed~~ supposed to eat or drink anything between sunrise & sunset – even water!

Muslim people use this month to think extra hard about how to live a better life that Allah (God) would approve of. I have tried to follow other cultures' traditions while on my journey, but I don't have to follow the rules of Ramadan, because:

1 I am not a Muslim and
2 I am on a journey!

Going on long journeys is so hard that you cannot manage without food, so you're let off all the normal rules. In other words, I need my banana sandwiches and water bottle at all times of the day!

The Arabic language

Arabic is extra hard for me because it doesn't use the letters that I'm used to, plus it's written from right to left (so 'hello' would read 'olleh'). Here are some words I have learned in Arabic. I got someone I met to write the letters out for me - I can't do it!

English	Arabic	How it sounds
hello	سلام	salaam
goodbye	مع السلامة	mah-ah-salaama
please	من فضلك	min-fah-dlak
thank you	شكراً	shoo-krahn
bicycle	درّاجة	dah-rahj-ah
food	أكل	ah-kell
water	ماء	mah-ah

0 1 2 3 4 5 6 7 8 9 = ٩ ٨ ٧ ٦ ٥ ٤ ٣ ٢ ١ ٠

Even though I normally count numbers out on my fingers, I wanted to learn what numbers look like in Arabic because I found out that's where our own numbers come from!

TOM AND MUMMY

After five months of pedalling, Tom had ridden from his front door in England to the Egyptian border. He was in Africa at last! His hair was long now and his clothes were faded by months of strong sunshine, but he was fitter and stronger than ever before. He could ride all day and then, tired but happy, sleep like one of the Egyptian mummies that he hoped to see. He had never felt so happy.

Tom rode towards the famous pyramids. But he first had to cross the Suez Canal. As he got near to it he was surprised to see what looked like ships sailing through the sand. Only when he was very close did he see the narrow strip of water that was the canal. It was not much wider than the ships that sailed along the canal in single file. It was weird to see a canal in the sand.

After the canal Tom pedalled into Cairo, the capital city of Egypt. The traffic was total chaos. Cars beeped at each other and motorbikes weaved through the traffic jams and delivery boys on bicycles and donkey carts with wobbly wooden wheels trundled slowly along busy motorways.

A baker cycled slowly by with a tray of loaves of bread

balanced on his head. He was covered from head to toe in flour and looked like a ghost.

Cairo had a skyline of tall modern buildings, mosques and minarets (the tall thin towers above mosques that are used to call everyone to come and pray). Above all the other buildings Tom suddenly spotted the clear outline of the famous pyramids. He had seen pictures of them in books at home and also learned about them at school.

So he was very excited to see the real things. Even the best photograph in the world is not as exciting as seeing somewhere with your own eyes. He pedalled quickly towards them. It was late afternoon and the sun was sinking down the sky, losing some of its ferocious heat.

Tom sat down in the shade of the Great Pyramid. The pyramids are the only one of the seven Ancient Wonders of the World still standing, and even today they are one of the most wonderful things on Earth. Like Baalbek and Petra it is hard to believe that the pyramids were built without modern machinery. Tom drank from his water bottle and made himself an extra large banana sandwich to celebrate having made it all the way to Africa.

The Pharaohs who built the pyramids were very, very rich. When they died they were buried inside their pyramids, together with huge amounts of gold and treasure. Most of the treasure has been stolen over the last few thousand years. So nowadays the small burial chambers are just an empty room deep within the heart of the pyramids. Ancient Egyptians used special techniques to preserve the Pharaohs' dead bodies. They wrapped them in long bandages to create mummies and these can last for thousands of years.

Tom's next adventure was going to be to cycle all the way down Africa from Cairo to Cape Town, the city at the opposite end of Africa. The continent sounded really exciting: elephants and crocodiles, drums and spears, big cities and empty wildernesses and so many different cultures and languages and people. His heart beat a little faster as he thought of all that awaited him.

MAN-MADE WONDERS OF THE WORLD!

I've seen so many wonderful sights already, but recently I saw two man-made things that have really impressed me.

Number one is the 100 mile Suez Canal, which links the Mediterranean Sea to the Red Sea. It saves a ~~distance~~ many thousands of miles for ships travelling from Europe to Asia and back. Before it was finished in 1869, trade ships from Europe would have to sail all the way to the bottom of Africa and back up the other side to reach Asia. This was a huge ~~ditour~~ detour and took several months. I bet the people on the ships were relieved when they didn't have to go around an entire continent any more!

The second thing is probably my favourite: the Pyramids! There are 138 pyramids in Egypt, but the most famous are the pyramids of Giza. They were built as tombs for the Pharaohs.

Egyptians mummified the Pharaohs' bodies when they died because they believed that if the body was preserved, then they'd live forever. Pharaohs were buried with massive amounts of treasure, clothes, food, furniture, and other items they would need in the after-life. If I had a pyramid tomb and got mummified, I'd choose to be buried with my computer so I could play games!

The Great Pyramid, made with two million bricks, was built for King Khufu. It is 140 metres high!! It was the tallest building on earth for 5000 years until the Eiffel Tower was built. Now that I have seen both, I think the Great Pyramid is cooler than the Eiffel Tower because there weren't any machines back then to help them move and stack the bricks - they weighed a massive two tonnes EACH!

THE BORDER GUARDS

Tom cycled through Egypt alongside the river Nile, the longest river on the planet. He was surprised by how narrow it was. He watched farmers ploughing their small fields. Their large wooden ploughs were pulled by oxen with big, curved horns. The fields are very good for growing crops as the river floods every year, adding a layer of nutritious mud to all the fields. The Nile is more than 4000 miles long, four times longer than the length of Great Britain.

Tom gulped nervously as he thought that not only did he have to cycle the whole length of the river, but he also then had to keep going for thousands of miles more until he reached Cape Town! Africa was huge, so he tried not to think too far ahead. His mind was busy enough planning the first big challenge of Africa: crossing the desert in Sudan.

Tom had never been to a desert before, he had only been to a beach. He could not imagine trying to cycle along a beach, never mind crossing a whole desert on his bike! The thought of all that sand did little for his appetite.

Everyone in Egypt told Tom he was mad to even think of crossing a desert on a bike.

"It is too hot!" said the man at the fruit stall in the market, handing him an extra banana to wish him luck.

"It is too far for you: you are too skinny to survive!" cried a large man who filled up Tom's water bottles for him.

"It is too sandy. You will have to push the bike!" warned a boy at a village mosque where Tom had been given permission to put his little green tent and camp for the night.

Nobody thought that he could do it. But Tom remembered everyone at home telling him that even getting to Africa on a bike was impossible, and yet here he was, still going strong. The only way he would find out if he could get across the desert was by trying it. He knew that he might not succeed and might have to give up. But it was better to try his best and fail than not even have a go.

Tom prepared carefully. He wrote in his journal a list of everything that he needed to do if he was to survive the dangerous desert crossing.

He was as well-prepared as he could be. Now he just needed to trust himself and go for it. Tom knew that it would be hot, hard, scary and lonely. But he thought of how happy he would feel if he managed to succeed at something that everyone had told him would be too difficult. It was worth having a go.

After a few more weeks cycling down Egypt, Tom saw a barrier across the road. The weather had grown hotter and hotter every day he rode south. The tarmac road was shimmering in the heat. There were no plants or trees. The air was hot and still. He had reached the border crossing into Sudan.

On the Egyptian side of the barrier a police officer asked to check Tom's passport. He was amazed at all the stamps that were in the passport already.

"You have been to 16 countries on this bicycle?" he asked, disbelief written across his face.

"Yep!" smiled Tom, "But I still have many more to cross if I am going to make it round the whole world on my bicycle."

"You are riding round the world? You are crazy, my young friend!" answered the Egyptian police officer, whose name was Sergeant Sharif. Sergeant Sharif was very short, and almost as wide as he was tall.

His face turned serious as he said, "You must not go into Sudan. It is a desert! It is much too dangerous." He beckoned Tom close and whispered in his ear, "And in Sudan ... they are all robbers! Every single person is a robber."

Sergeant Sharif pointed over his shoulder to the Sudanese police officer who was standing only a few metres away but on the other side of the barrier. He was staring off into the distance and whistling, pretending not to have noticed Tom and his bicycle.

Tom thought that the Sudanese police officer looked like a nice man, not a robber, but he promised the Egyptian that he would be careful. "Good luck!" laughed Sergeant Sharif as he raised the barrier and let Tom pedal on into Sudan. "You'll need it!"

Standing on the other side of the barrier was the man dressed in the uniform of the Sudanese police force. His name was Sergeant Amarri. He spoke Arabic, like the

Egyptian policeman, but they never spoke to each other. They did not like each other. As Tom rode round the world he often found that people did not like the people in the country next to theirs, even though they didn't know anything about them.

This seemed so silly. Those two police officers had been standing almost side by side, in silence, ignoring each other, for years. If they had chatted they would probably have become friends and their boring days standing on duty would have been more fun.

Sergeant Amarri pretended that he had not noticed Tom while he was speaking to Sergeant Sharif. Now he gave Tom a great grin of welcome. Sergeant Amarri was a tall, thin man with very dark skin. His eyes shone white in his face and, when he smiled, his teeth gleamed like a crescent moon. Sergeant Amarri seemed to be a very happy man.

"Welcome to Sudan!" he said. "Sudan is the most beautiful country in the world. You are very welcome here."

The Sudanese police officer stamped page 17 of Tom's passport with the Sudanese visa stamp. It was big and colourful and decorated with swirls of Arabic writing. He checked that Tom was carrying enough water.

"My friend, be careful in our desert. It is a difficult place. You must ration your water carefully."

Tom promised that he was carrying plenty of water, but in truth he was quite nervous. Everyone he had met recently had warned him about the desert. But Sergeant Amarri continued with words that quickly cheered him up.

"Our desert, called the Nubian Desert, is very beautiful. If you are brave and well prepared, then you will enjoy an experience you have never imagined before. You will see stars as bright as diamonds, sunsets that blaze across all the heavens. Nobody in your country will have seen what you will see by the time you reach the other side."

Then he beckoned Tom close, pointed over his shoulder to Sergeant Sharif on the other side of the barrier and whispered in Tom's ear, "Those Egyptian people – they are all robbers! You are lucky to have escaped that country!"

Tom explained how much he had enjoyed riding through Egypt and that the Egyptian police officer was actually very friendly.

Sergeant Amarri looked surprised.

"Young Tom, is this true?" he asked.

"Completely true," answered Tom. Perhaps a little untruthfully, he added, "And he told me how much he loved Sudan."

"Well in that case I should talk to this Egyptian policeman, don't you think?" said Sergeant Amarri.

"Definitely!" said Tom.

Then he waved goodbye and pedalled down the road.

Behind him he heard Sergeant Amarri turn to Sergeant Sharif and say nervously, "Excuse me, Sergeant Sharif? We have been standing next to each other for many years without ever once speaking. I thought that perhaps you might like to come over to my side of the barrier and join me for a cup of tea? I have many questions I would like to ask you about Egypt."

And before Tom had gone very far he heard the sound of loud laughter behind him. It seemed as though the two police officers had become friends already. Tom smiled and rode into the desert.

DESERT SURVIVAL

After listening to many different people talk about the desert, I came up with a list of golden rules for surviving it:

- <u>Collect</u> lots of bottles to put water in.
- <u>Fit</u> wide, knobbly mountain bike tyres to help grip in the soft sand.
- <u>Wear</u> a big sunhat, strong suncream, long trousers & a long-sleeved shirt to help protect against the sun.
- <u>Wear</u> sunglasses & a face scarf for protection against sandstorms.
- <u>Use</u> a compass to help keep on course.
- <u>Tell</u> the local police your route so that they can find you in an emergency.
- <u>Start</u> cycling very early before it gets too hot & try to find shade in the ~~middle~~ middle of the day.

As well as practical information, one of the things I've been told about a lot is how clear the stars are in the desert.

But they're not just beautiful ....

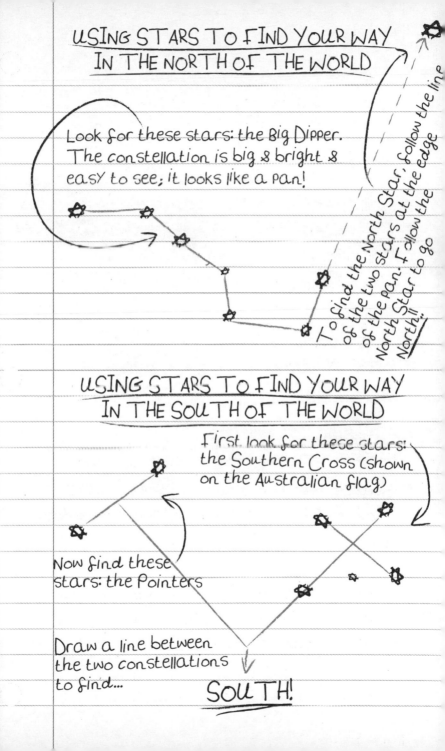

USING STARS TO FIND YOUR WAY IN THE NORTH OF THE WORLD

Look for these stars: the Big Dipper. The constellation is big & bright & easy to see; it looks like a pan!

To find the North Star, follow the line of the two stars at the edge of the pan. The North Star to go North!!

USING STARS TO FIND YOUR WAY IN THE SOUTH OF THE WORLD

First look for these stars: the Southern Cross (shown on the Australian flag)

Now find these stars: the Pointers

Draw a line between the two constellations to find...

SOUTH!

SAND AND SUDAN

An hour after crossing the border the road suddenly stopped; it was the end of the road. Tom would not see another proper paved surface for many months to come. He hoped that his bike would be strong enough to cope. He hoped that he would be strong enough to cope.

He rode off the smooth tarmac and into the desert. The desert! Silence. Heat. Flat, hot silence in all directions. He sipped from his water bottle, wiped sweat from his eyes, and began to ride. Instantly he was bouncing and shaking around, his bags were rattling and his speed dropped right down. Tom looked around. There were no tall sand dunes or camels like you would imagine you'd find in a desert. There was just a shimmering emptiness. So this was what a desert was like ... Wow!

Day after day he moved slowly over the flat, stony plains, or dragged his heavy bike through deep sand. He was hot and thirsty but he knew he had to keep going. He steered by his compass, heading south all the time. At night he laid his sleeping bag out on the sand (after checking carefully for scorpions) and stared up at the moon as he fell asleep.

At dawn, as the orange sun rose slowly over the horizon, Tom would pack away his sleeping bag, eat a handful of dates for breakfast (he had read a book about the Bedouin desert people, and they had always eaten dates), brush his teeth, and put on his shoes. Before he put his shoes on he had to remember to shake them out to make sure that no scorpions were sleeping inside. This was a funny habit to get into and Tom often forgot to do it. It was something he never had to do back in his normal life. But one day a big fat scorpion crawled out of his shoe while Tom was eating breakfast. After that he never, ever forgot to shake his shoes again!

Tom checked his compass, even though by now he knew that the sun rose in the east so that as long as he kept the sunrise on his left side then he was heading south, and off he went again. Another day had begun. He was making good progress across the Nubian Desert.

But Tom's bike was heavier than ever. His bags were rammed with food and bottles of water. He knew that he had to be very careful to make sure his supplies lasted. He had to save his water, so did not waste any washing himself or his clothes. He wore the same clothes day and night, which became crusty with salty sweat. His hair was knotted and tangled and his face was covered in dirt and dust. He was dirty and stinking and disgusting. And he loved it! This was adventure! This was the desert everybody had told him was impossible, but he was having the time of his life!

After three weeks, Tom reached a small town. He rode across the hot sand and back onto a road once more.

The road was only made from gravel, but after rattling through the desert it seemed very luxurious. It felt strange to be back in civilisation again: there were flies in the air and old cans and piles of rubbish lying in the streets. The silence was over; he heard engines and music and conversation. But what Tom was most fascinated by was to see people again. Sudanese men wear long, flowing white robes and the women wear beautiful, multi-coloured robes. As Tom walked through the village, looking for the central water pump where he could refill his bottles and wash his face, he could not stop staring at people. He saw fat people and thin people, tall people and short people, young people and old. He was fascinated how every human looks slightly different even though they all have two eyes, a nose, a mouth ...

Being on his own in the wilderness for a long time made Tom much more observant about normal, everyday things. He had loved the beauty and the silence of the desert and the successful challenge of trying to survive out there on his own. But he was glad to be back amongst people once again.

INTO ETHIOPIA

Arriving in Khartoum, the capital city of Sudan, Tom pedalled to a junction in the river where two mighty rivers, the Blue Nile and the White Nile, come together and become, simply, 'The Nile.' He followed the Blue Nile towards its source. The next stage of the journey had begun, as he pedalled into the mountainous country of Ethiopia.

The children in Ethiopia had never seen anything like Tom and his heavily-laden bike. When he rode through Europe people had looked at Tom carrying all his things in four small bags and thought that he must be a poor person. But in Africa people looked at Tom carrying so many things in four bags and thought that he must be a rich person.

As he rode along groups of 10, 20, even 50 young children would chase alongside to stare at his blond hair and marvel at his beautiful bicycle. Ethiopians are good long-distance runners, and so the children ran for a long way, even though Tom was on a bike. Tom thought of all his classmates back in England: none of them would be able to run as far or as fast as these children in Africa (and most of them did not even have any shoes).

Even though he was surrounded by many other children, Tom was feeling lonely. He could not speak Amharic, the Ethiopian language, and the children could not speak English. Tom was missing his family and his friends. He stopped riding, laid his bike down on the dusty earth, and sat down on the ground. A big fat tear fell into the dust. For the first time on his journey Tom wished he was back home.

The crowd of Ethiopian children stopped running. They stood in a silent circle around Tom. They could see that he was upset. But because they could not speak English they could not say anything to cheer him up.

Just then another boy came running across the fields from his home to see why the crowd had gathered. He was about the same age as Tom. His name was Abai. Abai thought that life in his village was really boring. Nothing exciting ever happened. As he ran, Abai tried to guess what all the people were looking at. He never imagined that he would find a blond English boy in the middle of the crowd!

Tom looked up as Abai pushed his way through the crowd.

"Hello," said Tom. He couldn't really be bothered to say hello because nobody could understand him, but his Mum always made him say hello to people. It was polite, she said.

"Hello," answered Abai.

Tom's head sprang up as though it was fixed to a spring. His eyes opened wide.

"Can you speak English?" Tom asked.

"Yes, I can speak English," replied Abai, shyly.

Abai's Dad was the local teacher. Just for fun and ever

since Abai was tiny, he had been teaching his son little bits of English. Abai had enjoyed learning the strange sounding words, but he had not imagined that he would ever actually meet a real English person. When he saw Tom sitting on the dusty ground in the centre of all the people, Abai was excited. But he also felt embarrassed. All the other children in the crowd were not staring at Tom any more, they were staring at Abai, amazed that he seemed to be able to talk to the strange boy on the bicycle.

"My name is Tom. What is your name?"

"I am Abai. Where are you from? What are you doing here? Why do you have a bicycle?" Abai had so many questions to ask that he didn't know what to ask first and he was not giving Tom any time to answer.

Tom smiled at the rush of questions and explained that he was from England. He was trying to cycle round the world. It always sounded like a crazy thing to say. But just then it sounded really, really silly as all Tom wanted to do was go home.

All the other boys and girls began shouting at Abai.

"Who is he? What is he saying? Can you understand him? Where has he come from? Is he lost? Why is he on a bicycle? What is in his bags? Why is he so dirty?"

Everyone was talking at once, wanting to know about Tom and his adventure. They were all laughing and smiling.

Tom didn't feel so lonely any more. He answered Abai's questions and then started to ask some of his own.

"Why can you all run so far? Why are you carrying spears? What did you think I was doing here?"

Abai explained that every day he and his friends had to travel many miles to get to the nearest school. But there was no school bus and nobody in the village owned a car, so they all had to travel on foot. Walking took too long so they would run instead. Running every day meant that everyone was fit and fast. They would also run back home again at lunchtime when school ended for the day.

Tom wished that his school finished at lunchtime. But Abai explained that in Ethiopia many children had to work in the afternoons to help their families earn enough money to buy food. That was why some of the boys were carrying long, sharp spears. They were supposed to be looking after their sheep in the fields, protecting them from dangerous wild animals. But the sight of Tom on his bicycle had been too much for them to resist. They had abandoned their sheep and come running along to join in the fun.

"Why don't you come and meet my family?" Abai asked Tom. "You can spend the night with us. And you can try some Ethiopian food, some *injera*!"

"Thanks a lot," said Tom. "That would be great. I am always hungry these days. And I would love to see your house."

So Tom waved goodbye to the crowd of children, who smiled and waved back. Then he pushed his heavy bike, helped by Abai, across the dry and stony fields. He was feeling much, much happier.

Outside the house was a small field with some vegetables growing in it. Abai's house was small and round with walls made from baked mud. The roof sloped steeply. It was made from bundles of long grass tied tightly together. Smoke was streaming through the roof. It looked as though the house was on fire!

"Don't worry," said Abai, "my Mum must be cooking. But she is not burning the food. We cook on an open fire in our house and it gives off lots of smoke. My Mum's a very good cook. You're going to love her food."

Then Abai shouted in a loud voice something in Amharic which Tom could not understand. Abai's parents, three brothers and two sisters all came out of the small house. They were very surprised when they saw Tom.

Abai explained that Tom came from England and was riding his bike all the way round the world. The family gasped in shock, and laughed, then eagerly took Tom into the house. He was a very unusual visitor. Abai told Tom that he was very welcome and that they had arrived at the perfect moment: dinner time!

One of the things Tom was enjoying most about riding round the world was trying so many different kinds of food. It was not always delicious but it was always interesting. And it made a nice change from banana sandwiches. Ethiopian food was one of the most unusual he had tried so far.

They all sat on the floor around a low, circular table. The family asked Tom lots of questions about his expedition. Abai or his Dad, the teacher, translated their questions.

Then Abai's Mum placed a large round tray on the table. It was covered with what looked like a huge pancake.

"This bread is called *injera*," said Abai. "In Ethiopia we eat it almost every day."

On top of the *injera* were heaps of stews and cooked vegetables. There were no plates or knives or forks.

Abai showed Tom how to eat in the Ethiopian style. He tore off a piece of *injera* with his hand and used it to scoop up some vegetables. He popped it into his mouth and smiled as he chewed. Next it was Tom's turn. The whole family watched Tom's face to see if he liked the food. Abai's Mum, who had cooked the meal, watched the most carefully of all. Tom tore off a piece of *injera* and began to eat.

After such an eventful day Tom was really hungry so the food tasted especially good. He smiled and said, "*Amesegenallo*," which means 'Thank You' in Amharic. He liked the food very much. It was very spicy.

Everyone laughed. They were happy that Tom enjoyed their food. Then the whole family began to eat together from the same giant piece of *injera*, sharing the food. Everyone was talking all the time as well as eating all the time. It was a very noisy meal. There were so many questions to ask and so much to learn about each other's countries. Abai's Mum was shocked to learn that people in England do not eat *injera*. And Tom learned that in Ethiopia it was actually a different year than in England! The Ethiopian calendar is seven years later than the rest of the world's calendars. Even telling the time is different. Rather than starting a day at midnight as Tom was used to, on Ethiopian time the day begins at sunrise. So one hour after sunrise is called one o'clock in the morning.

The house was very small so there was not a spare bed for Tom to sleep in. But that did not matter. He was very tired and was happy to just roll out his sleeping bag and sleep on the floor.

In the morning as he packed, Tom thanked his new friends for looking after him so well. As he cycled away, the family waved right until he had ridden out of sight, on towards the next new friends he would meet, and on towards the really steep roads of the Ethiopian highlands. Abai's kind family had really cheered Tom up and he was excited about his adventure once again.

For the next few weeks Tom rode through the mountains. The road was really rocky and bumpy, and his poor bike took a battering. Monkeys swung in the trees overhead, watching as Tom pedalled slowly past. The biggest mountains he had ever seen towered above and around him. And he had to sweat and pant his way up and over all of them. His legs ached each evening but he felt his muscles growing too. And the downhills were brilliant.

Tom definitely felt ready for a cool swim by the time he reached Lake Tana, Ethiopia's biggest lake. He had been told that there were crocodiles in the lake. But he was so desperate for a refreshing dip that he thought it was worth the risk. He only had a very short swim, just in case the crocs did decide that they were hungry!

After the dry Middle East, the desert in Sudan, and the rocky mountains he had just ridden through, Lake Tana seemed especially beautiful. Colourful bushes grew on the shore and green trees waved in the breeze. Pelicans flew through the sky and cormorants dried their wings in the sunshine before diving into the lake to catch fish.

Lake Tana is usually described as the beginning of the Blue Nile. From the lake this branch of the world's longest river crashes over a massive waterfall and then flows all the way down to the sea in Egypt. So Tom had now cycled the whole length of the river.

It was an important landmark. He treated himself to a banana sandwich in the shade of a big tree. As he chewed his thoughts turned to his next big adventure: crossing the equator and riding into the southern half of the world.

ETHIOPIA

I'm having a brilliant time in Ethiopia.
I've eaten meals with my bare hands
and I have seen palm trees, monkeys,
hippos and even a crocodile.

The food here is amazing. It is usually
very spicy, coated in a mixture called:

berbere

Any time food is shared, like injera, it
is really rude to take it with your left
hand. You always have to eat with your
right hand.

The national dish is called 'wot'. It is
stew made with different meats, and of
course, berbere. I like 'dabo kolo', which
are fried balls of dough. They are just
as good as doughnuts!

Coffee is the most popular drink in
Ethiopia. The head of the house makes
fresh roasted coffee for everyone
after a meal. It smells delicious!

The River Nile

I have been following the River Nile all the way down Africa so far. It is an important source of water and food for all the people who live near it.

Here are some facts about it:

- The River Nile is the longest river in the world - over 4000 miles!!

- The River Nile is made up of two rivers (The White Nile and the Blue Nile) which meet at Khartoum in Sudan.

- The source of the White Nile is Lake Victoria in Uganda.

- The source of the Blue Nile is Lake Tana in Ethiopia.

- There are crocodiles in the River Nile (be careful when going for a swim!)

- There are also hippos in some places!

BLOOD, MILK AND BANANAS

The days were scorching hot as Tom pedalled deeper and deeper into Africa. He cycled through Kenya and Tanzania. He was sweaty all the time, even in his tent at night. The refreshing swim in Lake Tana felt like a distant memory. The land was hot and dusty. Weeks would go by before Tom next found a nice clean river to swim in and wash his clothes in. Thorny acacia trees provided the only shade for rest, though he learned the hard way to not bring his bike near to them. Their sharp thorns punctured his bike tyres.

Cycling through Kenya and Tanzania felt like riding through one of the wildlife programmes that Tom used to enjoy watching on TV with his sister, Lucy. He thought of her sitting on the big old beanbag at home in front of the television. He laughed as he imagined her face if she suddenly saw him on his bike pedalling across the screen in the background of a nature programme!

Although he had seen elephants on TV and at the zoo, Tom could not believe his eyes when he actually saw one in the wild. It was a quiet evening. Tom was sitting outside his tent happily rubbing the dirt from between his toes. A big pan of noodles was bubbling on the camping stove. The sun was just starting to set. It was one of those brilliant red African sunsets you see on TV. Everything was peaceful.

Tom looked up from cleaning his feet. His heart thumped suddenly in his chest because walking across the grassland in front of him was a family of elephants! A father, a mother, and a little baby elephant. The "little baby" elephant was actually bigger than Tom's tent! He did not know whether to be excited or terrified. These were the biggest animals he had ever seen. They would squash him flat if they sat on him.

The elephants had not spotted Tom. So he moved very slowly to fetch his camera and take a photograph of this special sight. He couldn't wait to show Lucy this picture. She would be so jealous. This was one of the best things that he had seen on this incredible ride. He watched the elephants until they had walked out of sight far across the plain. He kept very still and quiet until they had gone. By now his noodles had cooked too long and were really soggy. But it had been worth it!

That night Tom found it hard to fall asleep in his tent. His excitement at seeing the elephants had slowly changed to worry. He thought to himself, "If there are elephants here, what other animals are around?"

Suddenly his eyes opened really wide.

"What if there are **lions**?!"

As soon as he thought about lions he was very worried indeed. After many months of cycling there was not a lot of fat on Tom so he didn't think that he would make a very filling lunch for a lion. And because he had not washed or changed his clothes for weeks he hoped he might be a bit too smelly to be very tasty. But he was not sure how fussy lions were with their food. He hid a little deeper down inside his sleeping bag. Of course his tent and sleeping bag would not provide much protection from a hungry lion but it made poor Tom feel a little better. He shivered nervously.

Tom normally loved camping, but he did not enjoy it that night. Every gust of breeze, every far-off sound made him jump. Every little noise began to sound like a pack of hungry animals sneaking up on him. He imagined huge teeth drooling and then crunching him up. He imagined a huge lion licking his lips after finishing him off, giving a happy, full-up, Tom-flavoured burp.

He was very happy to eventually see the sun rising.

The long night was over. Tom was exhausted. He dragged himself out of his tent, stretched, and looked around. He felt a bit silly, now that it was daylight, at being so scared in the night. It was just a normal sunny morning like every other day in Africa. Tom brushed his teeth and splashed cold water on his face to help him to wake up. That felt better. He treated himself to a double-decker banana sandwich for breakfast (that's bread-banana-bread-banana-bread) and climbed back onto the bike. It felt even better than usual to be riding quickly through the cool fresh air of the early morning.

Tom decided that he did not want to sleep out in the countryside in his tent again until he was away from all the big animals. It would be safer if he stopped in a village in the evening and asked permission to sleep there.

And that is how Tom found himself drinking the bowl of blood and milk in a village of red-robed Maasai warriors.

It is a ritual they carry out on very special occasions. The men's wrists and necks are wrapped round and round with beautiful bright beads. They carry spears and shields, like you see on the Kenyan flag. When Tom had arrived in the village after another long day's ride, he had not been afraid of the spears. He had actually been glad to see them: these men could definitely keep him safe from lions. Maybe he would get a better night's sleep than last night! He asked the village chief for permission to sleep in the village, explaining that he was riding round the world on his bike and that he was scared of lions.

"Of course you can stay here!" laughed the chief. "We are very happy to be able to help you on your long journey."

As well as elephants and occasional traffic, Tom shared the road with lots of other people on bicycles in this part of Africa. Children cycling to school, grown-ups riding to work, farmers carrying their vegetables or pigs to market. Many people had decorated their bicycles with coloured tape or tied bunches of plastic flowers to their handlebars. And they had musical hooters instead of ordinary bicycle bells. Tom also passed ladies in bright dresses carrying huge bunches of bananas balanced on their heads as they walked. They usually had a small sleeping baby strapped to their back as well. Often the ladies would smile and give Tom a banana or two as a small present. He would munch the sweet fruit as he rode or sit down in the shade of a baobab tree to enjoy it.

He followed a broad and winding river for several days from Tanzania into Malawi. It dropped down towards Lake Malawi, one of the biggest lakes in the world.

Rising up from the far shore of the lake was a ridge of steep mountains. The side of the lake that Tom followed was flatter. Tom breathed a sigh of relief, remembering how hard the mountains had been in Ethiopia. At night the sky was full of stars. They seemed so close that at times he would try to reach out and touch them. Tom would pitch his tent on a warm sandy beach and go for an evening swim. They were good days. The lake was blue and beautiful. It was so big that it looked more like a sea than a lake.

The villages in Malawi were made up of neat, thatched cottages with small vegetable gardens outside them. There were lots of rubber trees growing as well. Each tree had small holes cut into the bark. White liquid rubber oozed out and was being collected in plastic bottles. Villagers sold this rubber in the market. It would be turned into things such as balloons or welly boots which would then be sold all around the world.

Tom noticed something strange about some of the cars that passed him in Malawi. At first he thought he was seeing things. But no, some of the cars really did have big fish dangling from the wing mirrors! How strange! So he asked a boy for an explanation. The boy told him that people bought fish from Lake Malawi to cook for their families back in the city. But the cars were very hot inside because of the sunshine, and the fish would start to stink before they arrived home. So people hung them from the mirrors to keep the fish a bit cooler and to stop their cars smelling up.

But the fish were nothing compared to Tom's surprise when he came across cooked mice for sale as a snack! Children were standing beside the busy road with rows of cooked mice on sticks. These are apparently a popular and tasty snack. Tom looked at them in amazement. He tried to decide which he would prefer to try: a cooked mouse, or another snack he had been told about: a burger made from the clouds of flies that rise from Lake Malawi at certain times of the year and are caught by local people in big nets.

"Mouse kebab or fly burger?" Tom wondered to himself. "Mouse kebab or fly burger...?"

The decision was so difficult that in the end he decided to settle for some sugarcane instead. That was much nicer than eating a mouse! Sugarcane is the plant that sugar comes from. It looks like a fat bamboo cane. You bite off a chunk, chew it and suck the juices. It is like chewing a stick except that it is a stick filled with sweet, delicious sugar. It is somewhere between eating a stick and eating a stick of rock candy at the seaside. Once you have sucked all of the sugar from your mouthful of cane you spit out the woody mess that is left.

Tom couldn't think of anything better than a day's bike ride, a stick of sugar cane, a swim in a lake and a night sleeping under the stars. This was the life.

BAOBAB TREES

Baobab trees are my favourite African trees. They look <u>so weird!</u> A lady from a village told me a fable about them which I think makes them extra cool:

When God made the earth long ago, he was very busy. He firstly made all of the different animals, then he asked the animals to help him plant all the trees of the world.

The animals formed a line and God began handing out trees to them. Last in the line was the ~~hyena~~ hyena: he was late to arrive because he had overslept. The hyena was a very lazy animal who did too much sleeping. The only tree that God had left when the hyena reached the front of the queue was the funny-looking baobab tree.

The hyena was so angry at being given this silly tree that he marched away in a sulk. And because he was angry he planted the tree upside down on purpose. That's the way it still grows today; looking like an upside down tree.

Cool story, huh?

I'm near the equator now. The weather's getting hotter and hotter and hotter. I've noticed that days and nights are exactly the same length here. The sun also sets _much_ faster here than at home.

Last night I stared at the beautiful colours of the sunset and I could actually see the sun dropping downwards as I watched. Soon after the sun sets the sky goes completely dark!

THE END OF AFRICA

On and on rode Tom. Days and weeks and months passed by. At last he reached the border crossing into South Africa, meaning the bike ride through Africa was nearly complete. A South African police officer asked to look at Tom's passport. She was amazed by all the stamps in it.

"You have been to all these different countries on this little bicycle?" she asked, disbelief written across her face.

"Yep!" smiled Tom, "But I still have many more countries to cross if I am going to make it round the whole world on my bicycle!"

"You are riding round the world? On this bicycle? You are crazy, my friend!" said the police officer.

"I *am* riding round the world. But for now I am just thinking about making it to the sea at the bottom of your country. That will mean that I have cycled the whole length of Africa. Cape Town will be the end of Africa."

"What an adventure you must have had, young Tom. Please tell me all about it."

Tom smiled as he told the police officer, called Sergeant Tshosane, about the beginning of his trip – leaving home and riding to France. He told her about the River Danube, the cave homes in Turkey, the pyramids, the River Nile, about monkeys and lions and all the many, many adventures he had enjoyed in Africa.

Sergeant Tshosane's face turned serious when Tom finished telling his story. She said, "You are very lucky to have made it so far."

Then she beckoned Tom close and whispered in his ear, "Africa is very dangerous. I am surprised you did not die in all the countries you have ridden through."

When Tom heard this he burst out laughing. Sergeant Tshosane jumped back with shock. She was giving Tom very serious advice. It was Not Funny. Plus, she was a very important police officer. She was not used to being laughed at by a young boy on a bicycle.

"Why are you laughing?" asked Sergeant Tshosane. She looked quite angry.

"I am sorry," said Tom, although he still had a big smile on his face. "I am not laughing at you. You just really remind me of somebody I met in Egypt, long ago at the very start of Africa. His name was Sergeant Sharif. He said the exact same thing that you have just said. I think you would become good friends if you ever got to meet each other."

Then Tom cycled towards South Africa, leaving a very confused-looking Sergeant Tshosane scratching her head.

The end was close! But South Africa is a big country and he had a long way to cycle before reaching the sea. And first he had to ride over the highest road in Africa. The highest road in Africa (called the Tlaeng Pass) is in Lesotho, a small, beautiful country which is completely surrounded by South Africa. Tom rode deep into the mountains, climbing up steeper and steeper hills every day.

Many of the people in the small villages of Lesotho were wrapped in blankets and wore traditional conical hats on their heads. They needed the blankets because the temperature was falling fast as Tom climbed higher and higher. Tom's water bottle even froze solid one night! He had not expected that to happen in Africa. He did not have any gloves as most places had been boiling hot and he had not needed them. So Tom put his spare set of socks on his hands and used them as gloves instead. They were a bit smelly as he had not been able to wash them for many weeks. But at least they kept his hands warm.

SOUTH AFRICA

When I am tired or a bit fed up I grumble to myself about how big the world is, how slow my bike is, & how it's going to take years of riding to get round the world.

But on days like today, when I had some exciting downhills and enjoyed a dazzling sunset, I feel really lucky to have ridden all the way from my house down to near the bottom of Africa.

Slowly but surely I'm moving round the world. I'm proving those people wrong who thought I would not even make it down the street. I have nearly ridden all the way down Africa!! Looking back on all of the things I have accomplished so far, it is strange to remember that I still have so much to see and so much of the journey still lies ahead of me.

For now I am happy to sit here and watch the sunset over the ocean, knowing that I have only just begun.

Facts about the country of Lesotho

(Pronounced le-soo-too)

- Lesotho is completely surrounded by South Africa; it has no coastline.

- It has the highest lowest point of any country in the world.

- There are only 1.5 miles of railway line in the whole country.

- In Lesotho, many people wear conical hats called Mokorotlos.

- The two official languages in Lesotho are Sesotho and English.

- Lesotho means "kingdom in the sky" which makes perfect sense to me because...

- Lesotho is very, very, VERY hilly!

By now Tom was high in the mountains and he thought that he must be getting close to the highest road in Africa. He stopped to ask a lady. She was fanning the flames and hot coals of a barbecue made from half an oil drum. A row of corn-on-the cobs was browning gently on the grill. The smell was delicious. Tom, hungry as always, bought one from the lady. He munched the corn and asked her if he was near to the highest road in Africa yet.

"No, no, no, no, no," she laughed. "You have a long way still to ride, my young friend."

Hours later, after much more sweating and panting up steep, winding mountain roads, Tom stopped to ask a boy who was trying to catch fish in a racing, noisy river.

"Excuse me, am I nearly there yet?" asked Tom.

"No, no, no, no," he laughed. "You have a long way still to ride."

Tom kept riding.

Looking back over his shoulder he could see down, down, down so far. He was amazed how high he had climbed. The view across Lesotho was beautiful. He could see so far. But still he was not at the top.

Tom looked back down the valley he had cycled up. He was even higher than some birds he could see arching above the village far below him where he had eaten the barbecued corn.

When he was so tired that he thought that he could not possibly continue any longer, Tom stopped to ask a farmer.

The farmer was leading his flock of sheep down from the fields for the night.

"Excuse me, am I nearly there yet?" asked Tom.

"No, no, no," he laughed. "You have a long way still to ride."

The roads were steep and winding. Higher and higher he pedalled. He stopped to dunk his head in a refreshing cold stream, hoping that this might give him a bit more energy.

Then a truck overtook Tom. It was very old and rattled noisily. It was so full of big boxes that it was very heavy.

It was really struggling on the steep climb, just like Tom was struggling. As the driver drew level with the bike, Tom called up to him, "Excuse me, am I nearly there yet?"

"No, no," he laughed out of the open window. "You have a long way still to ride."

The driver beeped his horn, waved, and drove away up the mountain.

Sometimes things seem too hard. Tom was beginning to think that riding his bike up the highest road in Africa was impossible. The end seemed so far away. He was tired and his legs felt wobbly. His face was sweaty and shiny. His tummy was rumbling and empty. His lunch of barbecued corn seemed a long time ago now. He was exhausted. The mountain had beaten him.

But just as he was about to give up, Tom had a thought. In his head he saw a picture of himself in the playground back at school when everyone had been laughing at his crazy idea to try to cycle round the world. Back on that day, did he really think he would cycle all the way down Africa? No way! But he had come so far. How had he managed to come so far? By pedalling one mile at a time, then one day at a time, then one country at a time. He had not got this far by giving up when things got tough. And if he could ride all this way down Africa then he certainly could ride up this mountain, couldn't he?

Tom said to himself, "I won't give up yet. I will ride just one more mile."

And he did.

And after that mile he said to himself, "I won't give up yet. I will ride just one more mile."

And he did.

And then he said to himself, "I won't give up yet. I will ride just one more mile."

And before he finished that mile Tom saw the road flattening out ahead of him. He was at the top! He had done it! He was on top of the highest road in Africa. The air was cool and fresh. Mountains rolled away below him into the distance, stretching for miles and miles and miles. It was the most beautiful sight of his entire journey. He had done it!

Nothing could stop Tom now. He was going to make it to the end of Africa. He cheered and zoomed down the other side of the mountain. Faster and faster he flew down from the highest road, heading for South Africa. He grinned with delight as the wind ruffled his hair. It was downhill all the way to the end now ...

He smelled it before he saw it. The smell was clean and cold and salty. The sea. Then he rounded a corner and there it was in front of him. The sea! The end of Africa. At long last!

Tom freewheeled down the hill onto the beach. He squeezed the brakes and stopped his bike. He lay the bike down and stood staring at the broad expanse of blue ocean. Wowzers! He jumped up and down and shouted at the sky. He had done it. He had actually done it. He had ridden from Britain to the end of Africa. He ran down the sand and out into the cold, noisy waves of the Atlantic Ocean, not even stopping to take off his shoes and socks. He had never felt so proud or excited. This had been the best adventure of his life.

But Tom's journey round the world was not yet over. In fact the biggest adventures were only just beginning.

Here's a special sneak preview of
the next part of Tom's journey,
starting in South America:

THE
BOY
WHO BIKED
THE
WORLD

Part Two: Riding the Americas

ALASTAIR HUMPHREYS
ILLUSTRATED BY TOM MORGAN-JONES

PATAGONIA: LAND OF BIG-FOOTED GIANTS

"**A** laska: 17,848 km." Tom looked up at the signpost and sighed. Alaska was his final destination. And 17,848 kilometres sounded a very long way to cycle. It *was* a very long way – more than 11,000 miles, more than a third of the way around the globe.

It had been a thrilling moment when, after weeks at sea, Sailor Sam shouted, "Land ahoy!"

Everyone on the boat had turned to look; the first sighting of land is always exciting for sailors. Hills! Trees! Other people! They had made it safely across the Atlantic Ocean. Tom had waved goodbye to the crew and grizzled old Captain Horrocks, then climbed onto his trusty bicycle. It was time to ride! But when you spend weeks at sea, your legs get a bit wobbly. It takes a while before you can walk normally on dry land again. It's even harder to cycle. So Tom weaved and wobbled as he pedalled away from his friends on the boat.

Now, looking up at the signpost, the thrill of being on land was fading. There was just so much land! Tom's plan was to ride from the bottom of South America all the way up to North America and eventually to Alaska, further than he had ever cycled before. His legs felt tired just thinking about it. Surely a normal boy couldn't cycle that far? Tom wasn't a superhero. He wasn't really strong. He was just a boy.

The signpost was on *Tierra del Fuego* in Patagonia – Spanish for "Land of Fire". It got the name because the first European explorer to arrive here saw from his ship the campfires of the Yaghan people who lived here. The explorer's name was Ferdinand Magellan. He believed that the native people who could survive in this wild land at the very bottom of the world must be giants, at least twice as big as normal humans. The name "*Patagonia*" means "Big Foot": this was, Magellan imagined nervously, a land of giants with huge feet.

Patagonia ... The Land of Big-Footed Giants ... The Land of Fire ... This was going to be some adventure! Like Magellan, Tom felt nervous himself.

Patagonia is the land right at the bottom of South America. It spans two countries, Argentina and Chile. But the borders between countries were invented long after mountain ranges and mountain tracks appeared. So, for the next few thousand miles of his 17,848 km journey, Tom would be zig-zagging in and out of both Argentina and Chile.

He sat by the sea and ate a banana sandwich, thinking about the distance that lay ahead. Booming waves burst upon the pebble beach. The strong wind tugged at his clothes and messed up his already messy hair. An albatross – the bird known as the king of the oceans because of its three-metre wingspan – circled effortlessly overhead, gliding through the wild wind. Tom gazed out to sea. The cold grey-green water seemed to stretch southwards forever. There were no cities or trees or flowers across that ocean. Across the ocean lay only Antarctica and the South Pole. Tom could see why this tip of South America was described as the End of the World – *El Fin del Mundo*.

He looked up at the albatross. Albatrosses can fly the whole way round the world. The fastest one took just 46 days to do it: much, much less time than it was going to take Tom on his bicycle. Tom called up to the albatross.

"Good morning, Mr Albatross, Mr Albert Ross. Please can I call you Albert?"

He felt a bit silly talking to a bird, but there wasn't another person for miles and miles and miles. So he kept talking.

"Albert," Tom continued, "I'm on a journey round the world, just like you. I'm going to be the boy who biked the world. I need to cycle to Alaska and I'm really nervous. It's so far. I don't think I can do it."

Albert swooped down a little closer.

"I'll be OK, won't I?"

Tom probably imagined it, but he was sure that the great bird winked at him and waggled his wings as if to say, "You'll be fine, young man. Just get started – that is always the hardest part. Begin. Go! Go now, and find yourself a fabulous adventure!"

YOUR JOURNAL

It's a big world out there ... Where would you like to go & why? How would you get there?

YOUR JOURNAL

Plan what you'd take with you and what you'd leave behind, then draw a map of your journey.

YOUR JOURNAL

During your journey, what are the
main places you'd like to visit? Include
drawings of the landmarks.

YOUR JOURNAL

Write about a big adventure you have
had and include some drawings.

Acknowledgements

Thank you to Dan, Jenny and Martha at Eye Books for all their hard work on this book. Also thanks to Helen, Toby and to Tom (Inky Mess) for his lovely illustrations.

Hope & Homes for Children

Alastair has supported Hope and Homes for Children through his expeditions for over a decade. He has visited their projects in Europe and in Africa. He believes that their pragmatic, caring, efficient practices make a real difference in the lives of the young people they work with. Alastair became a patron of Hope and Homes for Children in 2010.

Hope and Homes for Children is a charity whose mission is to give hope to the poorest children in the world – those who are orphaned, abandoned or vulnerable – by enabling them to grow up within the love of a family and the security of a home, so that they can fulfil their potential.

Their vision is a world where every child feels loved.

To learn more or find out what you can do to help, visit their website: www.hopeandhomes.org

About Eye Books

Eye Books is a small independent publishing house. The team who works at Eye Books passionately believes that the more you put into life the more you get out of it.

Eye Books celebrates 'living' rather than existing. We publish stories that show ordinary people can and do achieve extraordinary things.

We are committed to ethical publishing and try to minimise our carbon footprint in the manufacturing and distribution of all Eye Books.

Follow Eye Books on Facebook, Twitter @eyebooks and our website www.eye-books.com

www.eye-books.com

eye books
Extraordinary Things Done by Ordinary People

About the Author

Alastair Humphreys is an adventurer, blogger, author and motivational speaker. He regularly visits schools to talk about his adventures.

Alastair's quest for adventure began young. Aged eight, he completed the Yorkshire Three Peaks challenge and at 13 he did the National Three Peaks in 24 hours! At 14 he cycled off-road across England.

At university, Alastair trained to become a teacher. But adventure took over! Alastair has now cycled round the world, raced a yacht across the Atlantic Ocean, canoed 500 miles down the Yukon River and walked the length of the holy Kaveri river in India. He has run the Marathon des Sables, crossed Iceland by foot and packraft, rowed across the Atlantic Ocean, and walked across the Empty Quarter desert.

More recently Alastair has been encouraging people to seek out adventure close to home. The 'microadventures' idea saw Alastair named as one of National Geographic's Adventurers of the Year.

Alastair is always blogging and tweeting about his adventures, big and small. Visit his website www.alastairhumphreys.com to see what he is up to and follow him on social media.